A

ANNA is for BELLE

By TASHA TUDOR

Checkerboard Press • New York

A is for Annabelle

Grandmother's doll

B for her Box

on the chest in the hall

C for the Cloak

we take out with care

D for the Dresses

we want her to wear

E for her Earrings

so quaint and so small

F for her Fan

to use at the ball

G for her Gloves

GANTS
DE MA POUPÉE

made of fine leather

H is her Hat

with an elegant feather

I is for India

whence came her shawl

J is the Jacket

she wears in the fall

K is for Kerchiefs

both frilly and plain

L for the Locket

she wears on a chain

M is her Muff

so warm and so cosy

N is a Nosegay

a bright fragrant posy

O is her Overskirt

worn with such grace

P for her Parasol

all trimmed with lace

Q is the Quilt

which covers her bed

R for the Ribbons

she ties 'round her head

S for her Slippers

to wear at the dance

T for her Tippet

the latest from France

U for Umbrella

with jet handle on it

V for the Veil

she wears with her bonnet

W—her Watch

to tell her the time

X is the letter

X is for Xerxes

The King

for which I've no rhyme

Y is the Yarn

her stockings to mend

Z is her Zither

and this is the end.

1 is One
by Tasha Tudor

Designed as a companion volume to Miss Tudor's popular alphabet book, *A Is for Annabelle,* this charming book includes numbers one through twenty. Each number is graphically illustrated by one of Miss Tudor's paintings and accompanied by an original verse.

A variety of pictures—of animals, children, trees and flowers—as well as the easy-to-remember verses will encourage the youngest readers to learn their numbers and make them want to return to the book again and again.

The old-fashioned loveliness of Miss Tudor's delicate illustrations make this a particularly inviting introduction to "how to count."